The Adventure Within

GETTING THROUGH THE MIRROR WITH NO REFLECTION

David Ladd

PUBLISHED BY CHENOA PRESS, HANSVILLE, WA

I would like to thank my parents for living their lives as one continuous adventure. I also want to thank my family, wife, son, stepdaughters, grandkids, and in-laws for being a part of my life.

Contents

Preface.. vii

1   The Adventure Within 1

2   What We Believe.................................. 5

3   Past Time.. 9

4   Harmony... 11

5   A Simple Relaxation Technique 13

6   Are Wizards Real?............................... 15

7   What is the Truth............................... 19

8   An Exercise to Feel The Truth................... 21

8   Choices... 23

10 The Boat, Energy and Me......................... 29

11 The Rock.. 33

12 Seeking Love 41

13 Expanding Awareness and Consciousness... 43

14 The Gift.. 47

15 If I Truly Care for and Love Someone 49

16 Secret Contracts................................ 51

17 How to Bring Energy into a Room............... 57

18 Energy Boundary Basics 59

19 Once Upon a Time 63

20 Spiritual....................................... 67

21 Poetry 71

22 In Closing 77

About the Author.................................. 79

Preface

The following pages are words that have come to me through times of contemplation and during the many days spent inside my sailboat cabin while anchored out in small coves in the San Juan and Gulf Islands. My main purpose in writing this is to share my observations on life with those of you who have questioned the meaning of life and existence itself as I have. I am also writing this to share with my family members and acquaintances who may be interested in knowing what has been going on inside my head for all these years. Since I tend to speak very little, it is rare for me to be heard expressing what I've written here. I am a self-confessed social hermit and spend much of my waking time alone, asking questions for which there may be no clear answers.

If you decide to read this, please know that I am not asking anyone to agree with me or to understand me. I am only expressing my inner thoughts and personal observations in my own quest to understand the purpose of life.

~ David Ladd
Hansville, Washington, 2019

"The perfect man has no self;

The spiritual man has no merit;

The holy man has no fame."

~ Chuang Tzu

THE PERSON WHO IS UNCHANGED
BY THE PRAISE OR CONDEMNATION
OF OTHERS KNOWS THE DIFFERENCE
BETWEEN THE INNER AND OUTER
WORLDS IN WHICH THEY INHABIT.

~

EVERYTHING IS AN ILLUSION OF MY
OWN MAKING AND MY ILLUSION IS MY
REALITY. THE ONLY WAY TO BE FREE
IS THROUGH THE MIRROR WITH NO
REFLECTION.

CHAPTER 1

The Adventure Within

A S HUMAN BEINGS, we have many universal traits. I believe that one of our most important traits is our desire for adventure. When children reach an age where they begin to become aware of themselves, even though they are not aware of what they are doing, they are beginning to seek adventure. They are looking, smelling, tasting, handling, rolling, crying, laughing, pooping, crawling, walking, etc. During and after puberty, the search for adventure becomes more complicated with the added layers of interpersonal and gender-related relationships.

Today's child, prior to puberty, may find adventure in books, video games, TV, movies, collecting cards, dolls, toys, and other indoor activities. My grandson is fortunate that his father offers him a healthy mix of indoor and outdoor activities, often taking him skiing, swimming, hiking, to karate, and on bike rides.

Throughout our lives, the quest for adventure is inherent in the nature of our normal growth. In each phase of life, we seek a new level of adventure. For some it may be nothing more than finding the next meal. For those who are not struggling for survival, it might be ski trips, travel, fancy cars, guns, or the perfect house and yard. As we pass into old age, our big adventure may be to find the bathroom because we can't remember where it is in the house we have lived in for 50 years.

A common thread in our lifelong searches for adventure is the search for something exterior. This is a search for something outside of who we are now that could somehow satisfy something inside of us that we are not even aware of.

If I ask a person what they are looking for in life, the first look on their face is often one of bewilderment because they aren't sure what I mean. They might respond with more money, a better house, a new car, a better relationship with their partner, or a new partner. When I repeat the question after saying "you have all that, but is that what you are really looking for," the person may get to a deeper answer, which is often somehow related to peace, happiness, or contentment.

So, when we come back to the idea of adventure, what are we really searching for? Is it really that thing "out there" that thrills us, placates us, or gives us some sense or feeling of being fulfilled? Do we feel like we must look outward because our senses—eyes, nose, ears, touch—are all external to us, because looking outward is the only way we have learned to examine life?

When we only look outward for adventure, money, a good car, or the perfect partner, we are not able to satisfy ourselves in a long-term way. When the adventure is over, we need to find another one. When the money runs out, we may lose the house, the good car, the perfect partner, and we are left worse off than before.

Do you ever remember hearing someone say that it is good to be "well-rounded"? I believe what is meant here is to be balanced in all respects. So, for all the time and energy that we spend looking outward for adventure or for the thing that might make us happy, we should spend an equal amount of time and energy looking "inward" at ourselves.

I am very fortunate to have had role models who made adventure a normal part of my life. I am also fortunate that I have had a modest income that has allowed me to go on modest adventures, buy modest cars, have a modest home, and lead a modest life. Along with all of that, from a very early age, I have also contemplated my inward existence and how my existence fits in with the outside world.

I was born in 1951, a time in which it was a rare person who had any idea what it meant to contemplate their inward existence. The word meditate was never spoken around me, but I still had an idea of fate and a sense of a higher power that existed beyond the understanding of normal human consciousness. Today, the words contemplate and meditate are common, although the actual practice of doing so is much the same as it always was because it is still easier to look outward than to look inward. I understand that it is also because most people don't have a clue about how to begin the work of introspection.

The best way to begin anything is to simply start doing it. How does the child start to learn about their outward existence? It is an adventure and they have fun. When you start to think of learning about your inward existence, look at it as "The Adventure Within," and make it fun. The goal of the child is to learn how to embody the outward expression of a human. The goal of the adult is to learn how to embody the inward expression of a human. The unconscious goal in both cases is to find and be peace, harmony, balance, and contentment.

Because we all run our lives differently, each of us will have a different way of finding the balance between our outward adventures and our inward adventures. I can only relate to you how I have worked to find my balance.

I took a mountain climbing course and for 10 years I climbed everything locally that I could. I traveled to many other countries where I climbed high elevation mountains. Amidst the thrill of the experience, I wondered about what could live at such rarified and cold extremes. I visited ancient ruins and cultural heritage sites and imagined what my life would have been like had I lived then. I scuba dived and imagined what the lives of the beings living below the sea level were like. For the last 15 years, I have often gone out in my sailboat for 3 to 4 weeks at a time. I have experienced the exhilaration of going from point A to point B; and the experience of sitting quietly down in the cabin for days at a time. During those times, I imagined the movement of the air and water currents circulating around me. I felt the wind and watched the tide as it went in and out. As I sit here now trying to come up with words to express my awareness, I look out the window and watch a tree as it maintains itself by drawing food and water from the soil, and by bending to the outside forces of wind and snow and the encroachment of the other trees around it.

CHAPTER 2

What We Believe

EVERYTHING WE BELIEVE, everything we think we know, all that we see and feel, and all of our conscious actions are based on our highest level of awareness. This is the level that our brains are comfortable with and have accepted as normal. This is the level at which we vibrate. This is where we are in our spiritual growth.

When we are born, we grow in physical stages that are visible to us and to those around us. These stages typically follow in a standard progression from birth to crawling, walking, running, interacting with others, and growing older. We move from one milestone to the next until we reach old age and death.

Ideally, our spiritual growth would follow our physical growth, and our level of self-awareness would be visible to us and to others. In this way, our spiritual growth would follow the same standard of progression from birth (rebirth) to death (returning to the cosmos). However, we humans are born with brains that do not want us to see ourselves for the brain's own protection. The brain wants desperately to keep us within our comfort zones. It can trick us—even create whole problems—to keep us prisoner to its own sense of comfort.

The brain also works in partnership with our subconscious.

During our growth in this life we invariably suffer emotional pain from our parents, our friends, and from unsuspecting others who are not even aware of the emotional pain they have inflicted on us. Our subconscious stores all of our unprocessed emotional pain, anger, fear, jealousy, hurt, etc., and can trigger these feelings to rise up and divert our attention from anything that threatens the brain's comfort. Often, the brain will choose to operate within a familiar emotionally based pain rather than disrupt its sense of comfort and control by making a change, even when that change may be for the better.

Along with our subconscious emotions, we also hold Karmic patterns that have been in place from lifetime to lifetime. These Karmic patterns might place us in repeated family, friend, and relationship dynamics, so that our behavior and our challenges throughout this life are the same as they have been in other lives. A Karmic pattern might be an irrational fear of crowds, water, or heights; or an overwhelming desire to be responsible, a healer, or a leader. We are always trying to clear our old Karma, while at the same time trying not to create any new Karma that we will have to clear in a later life.

We are faced with many challenges in this life. The first is to grow physically and to maintain a healthy body. The second is to grow emotionally and to cleanse and face all of our emotional pains so that our subconscious can no longer use them as tricks to prevent our growth. The third is to become aware of what our Karmic patterns are so that we can face and overcome as much as possible in this life.

To help us in this work, and to help us to become aware

of what is driving us, we can develop an understanding of the chakras - a system of energetic correlations between our physical bodies and our spiritual bodies.

To begin, we will consider the seven main chakras, which are the **Root Chakra, Sacral Chakra, Solar Plexus Chakra, Heart Chakra, Throat Chakra, Third Eye Chakra,** and the **Crown Chakra.** Each chakra represents a level of consciousness. As with our physical growth, we must understand each level of spiritual growth before we can obtain our full maturity. For most humans, up until the last 50 years or so, we have only operated with an awareness of the first three chakras. In the last 10 to 20 years especially, some humans have worked hard to move their level of consciousness into the fourth chakra - the Heart Chakra. One of the reasons people remember the Christ is that he lived from a heart-based level of consciousness at a time when that was not possible for others.

With the world as it is right now, there is a widening gap between those who are trying hard to just survive, and those who have let go of the struggle to survive. The person struggling to survive is living their life and making choices based on the lower three chakras of self-preservation, emotions, and will. Only when the person gives up the struggle to survive, stops being ruled by their emotions, and let's go of their will to be right, can they start to live in their Heart Chakra.

The keys to any growth are desire, education, practice, persistence, and the strength to let go of what we already know. To be stuck in what we know is to not allow anything new to be known.

Think and understand as much as you can. Write down any questions or things you want to think about in your life right now. After you have written down a sentence or paragraph, find a way to treat yourself. Think of a way to treat yourself that really rewards you for all your efforts. It is important to feel good about your new normal. Your body, mind, and spirit will respond better if it feels good, even if you don't think there has been any progress. Often, we will not even know that we have made progress because it can be difficult for us to track our own growth. It is important to believe there is progress even when we can't see it, and to reward ourselves at each step of the way.

We are talking about changing our patterns and seeing our lives from a higher and higher vantage point. After all, our behavior and what we know now are only patterns we have somehow established; and one that our brains try desperately to keep us caught in. We have the right and strength to change those patterns into ones that are better if we allow ourselves the chance to do it.

You can do anything you wish. You are a person with free will and only you are responsible for what you choose to believe.

CHAPTER 3

Past Times

I ALLOW EVERYONE THEIR OWN BELIEFS. A person may believe in some form of spiritual existence or they may not. They may, as did my parents, believe that their life on earth, as it is now, is all that they are given. But who among you really knows what your existence is? Are you aware of your consciousness now? Or are you just going to go through the motion's day in and day out until your tired body gives out?

Is there a meaning to your life? Is it just about how much fun you can have or how much money you can make? Is there an underlying longing for something that is just beyond your grasp?

I believe there is a place of peace, and that whether we acknowledge it or not, this is our subconscious driving force. But how can we find this place of peace if we have no point of reference or experience of it? How can we find something that we have never felt? You may have had an epiphany or some experience in your life that could represent this place of peace if you could only remember it. You could experience it through a spiritual awakening. However, it takes a slow and steady course of sober contemplation, meditation, and constant self-awareness to truly reach the place of peace. It requires you to be in harmony with everything around you, and harmony requires you to find inner balance.

I believe that finding the balance within oneself can take more than one lifetime, and I know I have had many. Since starting on my consciously aware energy healing adventure, I have had many unexpected visions and feelings about my past lives. During shamanic drumming journeys, Reiki guided meditations, my personal meditations, and while working as a healing guide to clients, I have seen through dream-like windows into my past and have also had some very clear and distinct visions. I have absolutely no doubts about who I am and who I have been. It is up to you to decide who you are and who you have been. Each of us must decide for ourselves who we are.

I have images of myself in the times of cavemen, running while hunting with a spear and being killed by a lion. I have been a trapeze artist in a circus in the 1820s. I have been a doctor, a psychoanalyst, an engineer, a serial killer (this could have been through committing ritualistic killings in the quest for immortality), a saint, a shaman, a high priest, and an energy healer. The only clear names I've had that I am aware of are Mureq, Da-Vid, and Paul. In every case mentioned, I can look back and see how my past lives have influenced my present life. I am now a compilation of everything I have ever been. In order to find our own balance, we must take into account all of who we are and somehow find the middle way.

Whether you believe anything I have said is not important to me. My hope is that by giving you these words, you might catch a glimpse of who you are so that you too can find your middle way.

CHAPTER 4

Harmony

TO BE AT PEACE, I must be in harmony with all that is. To be in harmony, I must first be in balance within myself. Be calm and still myself within. Reach out to the very edges, corners, and curves of who I know myself to be. Explore and accept my many faces. Come back gently to my center, to the place where I am balanced. My search for peace starts here, within the balance of all that I am. I strive to be the center from which point all things are balanced. The goal is to be in cosmic balance with who I am, when I am, and where I am in the voyage of my cycle of life and death.

As I age, I find that staying healthy has become a larger part of my mindfulness than it once was. Becoming more aware of and finding the balance between my body, breath, energy, and emotions is more important now than when I was younger. Qi Gong, which I think of as meditation in movement, helps me to do that. I have my own challenges, but I do my best to look at them as opportunities to expand my awareness for a greater healing of my soul's Karma. I take a long-term view of my existence in terms of lifetimes, which helps to change my perspective on my immediate concerns. Everything flows at its own pace. Rushing, pushing, and judging are of no use.

Picture yourself as a perfect, whole human being, no matter the state of your health. Simply picture yourself, in your mind's eye, as a perfect physical specimen. See yourself as being perfect in every way, a child of the universe.

CHAPTER 5

A Simple Relaxation Technique

T HE PURPOSE OF THIS EXERCISE is to open the right side of your brain. This is the nonverbal, feeling, intuitive side that you use whenever you are doing something creative.

Make a time and space that is quiet and comfortable. The room should be warm, and you might wish to play some meditation music. Sit comfortably with your eyes closed.

Imagine the most peaceful scene that you can remember. It might be a gently flowing stream, or a beautiful sunset. It makes no difference what it is, just as long as you find it peaceful and relaxing.

Become aware of your breathing. Take three deep breaths, exhaling slowly. Then consciously relax the muscles in your toes and feet. Once you feel they are completely relaxed, think about the muscles in your calves and thighs. Gradually relax all the muscles in your body, until you feel loose, limp and totally relaxed.

There is no time limit on this. The first few times you practice this you may find it difficult to relax completely, but in time you will be able to do it in under a minute.

Once you are totally relaxed, simply concentrate on your breathing. Imagine the oxygen coming into your lungs and being carried to every part of your body. Picture yourself as a perfect, whole human being, no matter the state of your health. Simply picture yourself, in your mind's eye, as a perfect physical specimen. See yourself as being perfect in every way, a child of the universe. Feel proud of yourself. Think of your achievements, and of your intelligence and creativity. Then, think about how your life will change once you are able to do what you are practicing.

Now, slowly stretch and open your eyes. The purpose of this exercise is to allow you to let go of all the problems and worries of your everyday life. It is very beneficial for you physically, as it allows every single muscle and organ in your body to totally relax. After this exercise, you should feel alive and full of energy. This will be reflected in your aura.

CHAPTER 6

Are Wizards Real?

WHAT IS YOUR ANSWER? What would you like to believe? Are you just curious or would you like to have some special power?

Well, the answer is YES. There really are wizards and it may surprise you to find that you know some of them. You might be surprised to realize that your siblings, parents, friends, relatives, neighbors, workmates, and the strangers you run into could be wizards. What may surprise you even more is to learn that everyone is a wizard. Everyone has a special power.

I believe that we come into this world with our power already determined for this life. Even if you don't believe this is true, it is clearly evident the first thing a newborn learns is how to get what they want. It certainly doesn't take long for an infant to find their particular way to manipulate others as a survival tool.

Maybe we should ask the question, what is a wizard? Is it someone who can fly, stop a speeding train, bend air or water, part the Red Sea, or manipulate the elements in some way? If a wizard is someone who can manipulate energy, then we are all wizards. Have you ever felt the emotions radiating off someone? Could you feel other people's anger, love, hatred?

When an angry person walks into a room, can't you feel it?

As with any learning process, there are many developmental stages of wizardry. As an infant develops in the womb, it turns, kicks, and grows until it is forced out into an unknown world. When a baby senses some discomfort—due to hunger, a dirty diaper, or a separation from its mother—its normal human reaction is to cry out. Hear me, it says, I am not feeling like I did before. If the infant gets a feeling of comfort after crying out, it shouldn't come as any surprise that they cry out again and again when they want something. It shouldn't come as any surprise either that an infant will cry out or whine to get what it wants for as long as parents allow it. If and when a parent does finally convince the child to stop crying or whining to get what it wants, most children will try different methods to get what they want. If they find a method that works, the person may continue to use that method their whole life and not even consciously realize that they are doing so. When their manipulative method becomes a habit, it becomes their subconscious normal operating procedure and an automatic response for their survival, whether for the preservation of their physical or ego self.

What happens when a person becomes aware of their special power? To be conscious of your power and to then use that power for the good of others as well as yourself is a positive step toward raising your consciousness. Sadly, many at this stage will use their power for their own benefit at the expense of others. And even more sadly, there are some who, with intentional awareness, will use their power to inflict pain on others. The angry person wants to infect all those around them with anger. And it is the same for all emotions. The emotional energy of the person radiates out to influence any and all other energies they contact.

> *It was a strange dream that these wizards cherished. They sought to make themselves beloved of those they cared for and to revenge themselves on those they hated; but, above all, they sought to become greater than the common run of men and to wield the power of the gods.*
>
> ~ Somerset Maugham, *The Magician*

Of course, to wield the power of the gods and to use that power for negative and selfish reasons can be disastrous for the person wielding their powers in the long run. Sure, in the short term a person can satisfy themselves with their gains and vengeances, but the law of energy will surely come at a great price to them. As the old saying goes, "those who live by the sword die by the sword." What these people don't realize is that while their power is a strength, it can also be their vulnerability. When another wizard is conscious of their own power and advanced enough to recognize the power and vulnerability of another wizard who is attacking them, that knowledge can be used to trick the attacker. When a person plays the "victim", they will almost always find a way to victimize anyone who they have trapped into treating them as a victim. So now the "victim" becomes the "victimizer". I have personally had my vulnerability used against me, and I have personally used another wizard's vulnerability against them. When you can "see" this and understand what has happened, it is quite an eye opener.

The only way out of this stage of wizardry is to understand your own power and your own vulnerability. The cleaner a person's emotional and Karmic life is, the less likely it is that they will want to use their power for selfish reasons, and it becomes far less likely that they will be vulnerable to someone else's power. The more self-awareness a person has, and the higher their level of consciousness, the more likely it is that they will use all of their powers for the good of others; and the less susceptible they become to being tricked or trapped by others. Know thyself and you will understand the mind of man.

The highest stage of wizardry is when a person is pure of heart and soul. Their very thoughts and imagery are manifest, and no harm can come to them.

I will leave you with some questions. Do you have a special power? Do you know what it is? Do you see how you use your power for selfish goals? Can you imagine how you could use your powers for unselfish goals?

CHAPTER 7

What is the Truth

*The truth is what we believe it is. We see what we expect to
see. We hear what we expect to hear. We react to others as we
believe they are acting towards us. To change our truth, we
would have to imagine and to believe in the truth we
wish to have.*

*A person who believes what they know is the truth and what
they think is right, is only expressing what their personal
truth is at that very moment.*

WHO KNOWS WHAT THE TRUTH IS? The fact is, the
truth is only what I believe to be true now. It is merely
where my brain has stopped its accepting process. The truth is
what I wish it to be. If I think I know the truth about someone,
it is only to the extent that I know the truth about myself. If I
assume I know the truth about someone and I don't want to
talk to that person about it, then I am unwilling or unable to
accept any other or deeper truth at that time. To protect itself,
the brain and/or the ego must hold on to its truth. Truth is an
evolving consciousness. There is no end to it. It is unfathomable and unimaginable to us at our present stage. Only when

given epiphanies, after a harsh struggle, or after facing it, am I allowed to accept the evolved truth. If the truth is what I seek, then I am in it for the long ride, through many lifetimes. The absolute truth may be unattainable in human form. This does not mean I should stop seeking it. But in the meantime, I will open my heart, love all living things as they are, and allow them to be proud of their truths. I will do my best to accept, honor, and love all things.

CHAPTER 8

An Exercise to Feel The Truth

BEGIN BY SITTING COMFORTABLY IN A CHAIR. Close your eyes, take four deep breaths, and try to relax as fully as you can. Now think about something you love, something very simple, like a color, a flower, or a food. Tell yourself, "I love..." Repeat it. Experience in your body what it feels like when you tell yourself a truth. Now get up and do something else for a few minutes. If you're at home, do something around the house. If you're out, walk around for a few minutes. Then come back, sit down, and close your eyes. Take four more deep breaths. And now tell yourself a lie. Say to yourself, "I hate..." (the same thing you just said you loved). Repeat the phrase "I hate ..." and try to experience what your body does when it hears a lie.

When you hear a lie, where in your body does it feel different? Do you feel a tightness in your chest or solar plexus, or do you see a particular color in your mind? Is there a "red flag" in your stomach? If you are trying to make a decision and your mind won't stop interfering with its chatter, say to yourself what you are about to do out loud. How does it feel in your stomach? Do you feel your "red flag?"

When you hear the truth, do you experience a warm sensation somewhere in your body, goose bumps or tingling sensations, a general peace, or does your heart "feel good?" Is there a particular color for the truth?

Repeat this exercise as many times as you want to until you know in your body what is truth and what is false for you.

CHAPTER 9

Choices

*The only person I have ever truly struggled with is myself,
and even that was all in my head.*

*If you truly want change, you must have willingness,
awareness, acceptance, empowerment, and focus.*

*Without some pain or discomfort, we go nowhere.
I know how difficult it can be to experience pain and
upheaval, but if we can look for anything that leads
toward a positive direction, even in trying times,
then we help to expand the collective consciousness.*

*Our emotions are often expressed outwardly, but the
root or seed of our emotions comes from within.*

*It is much easier to carry seeds of anger, hatred, sadness,
jealousy, and intolerance within us than it is to carry peace,
love, joy, forgiveness, tolerance, and acceptance within us.*

HOW DO WE MAKE CHOICES? What do we use to inform us when we make a choice? How can we ever hope to make positive changes in our lives if we don't think about and understand why we make our choices?

What choice did I have?

Many of the people I have talked to have asked me, *"Well, what choice did I really have?"* As if they had no responsibly for the choice they made. The truth is that as humans we always do have a choice. We have *free will* and we alone are responsible for each and every choice we make. But, to understand why we make our choices, it is important to contemplate the driving forces behind our choices.

Whether a person makes a choice instantly based on a gut feeling or the person spends a long time analyzing all the potential choices, it usually still comes down to some combination of the following driving forces: survival, human urges, ego, heart-based emotions, heart-based positive intuition, and spiritual knowing. Our choices also are predetermined based on our core emotional state. If a person has anger as their predominate emotional state, it is pretty much guaranteed that their choices will perpetuate more anger. If a person lives in a state of chaos, their choices will just make more chaos. If a person lives in a state of victimhood their choices will only confirm that they are victims. Only a person who lives in a balanced emotional state and a state of positive outcomes will make choices that are most likely to continue their positive state.

Survival

If an independent, unbiased, all-knowing person were to look at our lives up to this point, and this person was to tell us all the reasons for the choices we have made, what do you think those reasons would be? I would say that 98% of all our choices we make are for the survival of our physical self, families, children, tribes, our egos; the biological compulsion for sex; the need to dominate; be in control, or be submissive; anger, hatred, jealousy, or greed; and the beliefs in inadequacy, or superiority. Unfortunately, most people get into a habit of using a negativity-based belief system to make their choices, and of course their choices are never going to be good ones. If we asked a person what they based their choices on, they may say that they are seeking peace, comfort, balance, or just a feeling of contentment. But, if they fail to see the underlying negative forces that are behind their choices, they will be unable to make the positive choices that will bring them closer to what they seek.

Intentional choices

So how can someone start to make positive choices? We must start somewhere, and it is usually by taking an intentional and honest look at ourselves. When we know deep down underneath our conscious mind that what we are saying is only to protect our ego, or to manipulate, or to get what we want, we must become more honest with ourselves. We must start to take responsibility for ourselves and not blame others or the situations that our choices have gotten us into. We must investigate the core of our beings and examine what is in there. Is the seed in our heart one of anger, greed, jealousy, insecurity, superiority, hatred, or is it love? The seed that resides in our heart will come out in a flash when we are threatened in any way. It is our way, the habit we developed for survival. Only through meditation, quiet contemplation, and honest examination of our innermost selves will we be able to see what is inside of us. And even when we become able see our habitual reactions, like the flash of anger that can come out in a millisecond, we must still be willing to find the underlying cause of that anger and work to change our response over time. When we become able to observe our anger, we can start to discern between when we need it for survival and when we do not need it as a self-defense mechanism.

Letting go

Our choices are ours to make. We are totally responsible for our choices and the outcomes that come from them. We must learn who we are and take ownership of our lives. We do not have to stay in the ruts and habits that allowed us to survive in our childhoods. We do not have to die with anger in our hearts. We can give our hearts what they want only when we hold the seeds of forgiveness, allowance, tolerance, acceptance, and unconditional love for ourselves and others. However old we are and whatever we think are the reasons we must make the choices we made today; we always have another chance to make better choices tomorrow, right up until our last breath.

Years ago, during a healing session, I was asked if I could let go of my anger. My response was, *"If I let go of my anger, who would I be?"* Over the years I have had many thoughts about this. The following are some of those thoughts.

Can I let go of sadness? Can I let go of the grasping and grief for the loss of love? Can I release the anger and pain that resulted from the love that was denied me for unfathomable reasons? Can I become a person who is no longer actively searching for anything outside of this self while still feeling a longing for something that is richer and deeper, something that nourishes and complements the heart and soul? Longing for that fertile soil of pure love that will allow my spirit to grow freely and soar to heights unimagined. Longing for that which will not only bring joy into this life but will allow this whole being *to be the joy* that has lain hidden deep within for so long.

Honesty

For there to be any chance of growth, there must be a willingness to be vulnerable; to be *honest* about ourselves; to share without fear or expectation; and to love, value, and appreciate ourselves with an inner strength that does not depend on the thoughts, feelings, or judgment of anyone else.

How can we be the vibration that we seek if we have no concept of what that vibration feels like? If we don't know what the vibration is that we are seeking, we must bring forth the closest vibration that matches what we seek. Slow but determined steps lead to that which we are already. Peace and love within.

CHAPTER 10

The Boat, Energy and Me

My boat is the vessel of my body.
My body is the vessel of my soul.

The size, shape, and age of the vessel I inhabit are
of no consequence and are mostly for show.
The strengths, weaknesses, and flow of energy
within my vessel are who I am.

There are currents of energy flowing above, below,
and all around me at all times. How I navigate
through these currents is my journey.

When out to sea in my boat:
The sun shines on all other boats the same;
The rain falls on all other boats the same;
The wind rushes by all other boats the same;
The sea current carries all other boats the same
When "I" am in my boat when my boat is out to sea:
"I" can be angry at the sun for being too hot, or

"I" can be angry at those other "I's" for liking the hot
sun, or "I" can put on a hat, or "I" can decide to like
the hot sun.
Attitude and ego can determine emotions
if you let them.

SITTING IN MY LITTLE BOAT, my self-contained cocoon, being still, reading, trying to keep my body still and restrain myself from peering left or peering right, I am acutely aware of the constant stream of things moving around me. People and pets walk up and down the pier. Birds and fish head off in seemingly random directions. One layer of clouds drifts to the east while a higher layer of clouds seems to stand still. All is moving. My little boat rocks and pitches with the slightest flow of wind and waves. My heart beats with the air moving in and out of me. My blood pumps out and in, up and down. Where is the stillness? Where is the peace and harmony of life on earth? It must be within my heart and soul. It must be within my own mind. Everything outside—movement, sound, voice, action—is a distraction, or an excuse for inaction.

The air and water seem so calm and still around me. The fog fills the space where clear skies had been. I hear sounds of birds squawking, their wings flapping and slapping the water. A distant foghorn from a ship is calling a warning. The water is alive with random and chaotic flashes of silver as a school of small fish swarms below the surface. I sit, I wait, I listen, but what part do I play in all this? It is only my vessel that touches the water. Who am I, sitting here?

I sit inside my boat's cabin with my prayer flags and meek possessions. When I go from port to port and from cove to cove nothing changes except for the outside scenery. I am still who "I am," unless by some experience along the way, the "I am" within me awakens. Then everything changes.

The surface of the sea is constantly changing with climatic conditions. It can be wild and choppy when the wind and the currents fight each other, but the bottom of the sea is always calm and still, undisturbed by its surface activity.

When my boat moves through the water, it creates a wake. My boat has a deep keel and glides through the water, so its wake is minimal. As I sail through life, I want my wake to be as minimal as it can be.

At times there may be strong winds and currents pushing my boat around. With its deep keel and my steady hand on the rudder I can steer my course.

I lift the anchor from where it has been firmly planted in this cozy cove. So still and calm, there are no waves, not even a ripple. No bangs, clangs or any of the other noise's we humans make. Only the sounds of nature, of birds making their sounds from close by. No matter that I can only see a short distance because the fog has encircled me. I am in the center of my own universe. My boat cuts the smooth water and glides out of its area of comfort, past the entrance of this place, into the wide and mysterious water. Out here the sea is no longer calm. My boat moves forward through the the high rolling waves as the choppy sea moves in a direction of its own, its current flowing beneath me. The wind is off my starboard bow, pushing the waves higher as the current and wind fight each other. I have no qualms about my choice to lift anchor. I have no doubts or fears. Is this confidence or just the action of my plan? I hold on and look out into my sphere of vision. I can only see a short distance in any direction. My constant awareness is my only security. My awareness wanders to thoughts of my brother Steve as he heads out into the Atlantic from somewhere in South America in his 21-foot canoe shaped sail/row boat. What are his chances of survival? I know mine are high. I will make it home in a few days. Will Steve reach home again? I know my mother must be in mortal fear for Steve and she needs me there to hold her and dad together. Their once strong and adventurous life is hanging on by thin threads of energy that are growing weaker. My awareness comes back to focus as I sight a rocky shore that I must navigate to find my way through the narrow entrance of a small cove where I will wait until the water's current will allow me to go through Deception Pass.

CHAPTER 11

The Rock

IT IS NATURAL FOR US TO ASSUME that our perspective is shared and understood by everyone and everything else. But our perspective is unique to us. Everyone and everything has their own perspective. Can you imagine the perspective of a bee, spider, mouse, or even a blade of grass? When we interact and communicate with others it is important to consider what their perspective is if we are to truly understand each other. The story of The Rock is an example of a perspective that is no less important than any other. If we humans do not interact with Mother Earth from its perspective, we may not get another chance to learn this lesson. I wrote the story below as an example of seeing the world from the perspective of a large rock that sits on the shoreline near where I live and walk with my wife.

Somewhere in the far North on the continent of what we now call America, there was a large and very unusual mountain. This mountain was different from the other mountains around it because it had an awareness of itself and its surroundings. The mountain had no name, nor did anything else, for there were no humans or other beings that felt the need to name everything. The mountain had a contented existence. It loved the daily routine of the morning sun hitting its peak and slowly warming its way down to the base and all the surrounding hills and lush green valleys. It loved the changing colors as the sun shifted day to day from high summer to fall, from fall to winter and its long rest. It especially loved the feeling of spring when everything changed back to the lush green and colorful flowers. What a sight to behold from its lofty perch on high. The mountain's routine had gone on for so long that it didn't think anything else could exist.

Life was good for the mountain until one day it noticed that the normal patterns of the weather were changing. The periods of rain were getting longer. The summers were getting hotter and its snowy caps were melting. The melting snows were overflowing the rivers and the once lush valleys were flooding. All the plants, trees, and animals in the valleys were leaving. It was a lonely time for the mountain, but it still had itself.

Because the mountain was just a mountain, it didn't keep track of time. It didn't know how it had come to be where it was, but it somehow knew it was old — hundreds, maybe thousands or millions of years old. Now things were changing, and after what seemed like a short time, the waters of the valley were coming up its sides. Every day the waters rose higher and higher until its peak was almost covered. One day, it noticed that something cold was creeping up its sides as well. The waters were becoming solid and turning to ice. Because the waters had been seeping into its cracks, when the ice formed and expanded, chunks of the mountain began breaking off and rolling down its sides. Most chunks were small, but some were large.

The mountain didn't know it, but this was to be the start of a very long period of change. The land all around the mountain had turned to ice and snow. All it could do was watch as the sun dimmed and the ice and cold became its new world. There were no more seasons. No more birds. No more lush green meadows and valleys with small animals playing in the grass. But the mountain was still the mountain, and it stayed where it was.

What the mountain didn't know, because this was something that had never happened before, was that it could still feel all the chunks of itself that had broken off from it. As the ice was forming on the colder side of the mountain, it pushed more ice toward the warmer side of the mountain. This caused more chunks of the mountain to break free and roll down onto the ice flow, where they were carried with the ice in the direction we now called "South". The mountain could feel those parts of itself getting farther and farther away.

The chunks of the mountain that were being pushed south. Day after day, the chunks of the mountain that were being pushed south could feel themselves slowly moving farther and farther away from the mountain. But, because they were moving, their sense of time was faster than the mountain's, which was securely connected to its earthly foundation. You could almost say that they were much like our human children forced away from home and on their own adventure.

After many hundreds of thousands of years, the mountain's lost pieces could tell that they were slowing down and that the ice that carried them was shrinking. One day they noticed that they had stopped moving altogether, and the ice that had brought them so far from the mountain was melting and moving back in the direction it had come from. As the ice receded, some chunks found themselves high up on dry land. Some of the smaller chunks found themselves spread out over barren flat lands. One chunk, which was not too small and not too big, found itself just at the water's edge at the end of a long peninsula of what is now called the Puget Sound. This chunk of the mountain, for lack of a better name, was to be called "the rock".

The rock found itself alone amongst the very small chunks of the old mountain and the sand that made up the beach at the water's edge. It soon became used to its stationary existence, spending its days watching as the water's tide moved in and out and the sun rose and fell. One day, after many hundreds of years had gone by, the rock noticed some small fish nibbling at the green stuff that had started to cling to its sides. Many years later, it noticed small animals peeking out of the thick shrubbery and walking along the shore. The rock was enjoying its life, and always looked forward to the next sunrise. It often thought of the mountain and wondered if the mountain was enjoying its life too.

The rock had been a rock by the shore for a very long time and was used to the usual patterns of the nature around it, so it was very surprised when something strange and new happened. A long thin object floating on the tide came in from the water and landed on the beach right next to the rock. Three things stepped out of this long thin thing and, using only two legs, they walked up the beach and into the trees. The rock had never seen a canoe, and up until that point, it had only ever seen small four-legged animals. It wondered what these new creatures were.

After a time, many more two-legged animals arrived on the beach in more of the long thin objects that floated on the water. Soon these two-legged animals were spending much of the day on the beach next to the rock. The rock noticed that they had built structures from the trees that used to be growing along the beach. They began to stay overnight in these things they had built. Now there were many noises, fires, and activities happening all around the rock, but it could only watch.

After many years had gone by, the rock noticed that the old two-legged animals had gone, and a different kind of two-legged animal had come out of the trees. Soon there were lots and lots of these new two-legged animals that walked by the rock, usually without seeming to notice it. These new two-legged animals would come to the beach almost every day and most often, they would just walk on past it. But sometimes, as they passed, they would say things like, "what a wonderful rock!" Some of them would pick up small bits of things from the beach, and at times some would stand along the shoreline throwing little objects tied to a stick by a thin line out into the water. The rock had no concept of what the fishermen lined up on the water's edge were doing.

The rock noticed that some of the two-legged animals came close and talked to it. One day the rock noticed that one of them, who it recognized from other visits had brought a much smaller two-legged animal with him. Both creatures began coming together to talk to the rock. Because the rock was so aware of changes, it observed that over time, the smaller two-legged animal was getting bigger. After many years of visits from this pair of two-legged animals, it noticed that the bigger one was becoming old and bent over, while the one that had been the smaller was now big and tall. After a while, only the smaller one came to talk with the rock. This two-legged animal came for many years by itself, and then one day it came with another small one. After many years, the same thing happened to these two two-legged animals. The bigger one became old and bent over and the smaller one grew big and tall. The rock wondered if this was some new pattern in its life.

The rock had now been in this place by the shore for a very long time. It knew the patterns of the sky and the ins and outs of the water that it had watched over the many thousands of years since it was carried to this spot. It started to notice that the air was becoming warmer and it was aware of the exact day that it felt the water begin to rise along its sides. It knew that something strange was happening.

It noticed that there were very few two-legged animals coming to walk by it now. Then one day, it felt the air around it getting colder. After some years had gone by, the rock felt something very cold and hard creeping up its sides. The water had turned solid and was no longer able to flow. This new cold stuff that used to be water was growing thicker and higher on its sides, until it covered the rock entirely.

The rock had spent its days watching and feeling all that had gone on around it for so long that it had forgotten all about the mountain. Now, with the ice rising up its sides, the rock remembered the mountain and found that it could still feel a connection to it. The rock and the mountain are still there to this day, connected in a way that the two-legged animals can barely imagine. One day the ice may melt, and the mountain and the rock may see the blue sky around them. One day there may even be more two-legged animals around them. One day those two-legged animals may learn to appreciate the rock and the mountain and understand that without the Earth, they would have nothing to stand on.

"Think of yourself as a growing plant. A plant puts forth beautiful blooms when it has the energy to do so. The more it is fed, the less energy it needs for growth. If at any point your growth requires too much effort, try to find the needed nourishment. This is your responsibility. The river of life will take you to many places, but you must feed yourself along the way."

~ *A Fall to Grace*, Lao Tzu

CHAPTER 12

Seeking Love

I have known you and loved you from the beginning.

IN CHAPTER ONE WE TALKED ABOUT our unconscious goal to find peace, harmony, balance, and contentment. Underlying our goal is an ingredient that without it we may never reach our goal. This special component is the feeling of Love. We are all looking for love, but do we really know what that means. We all want it, need it, feel lonely without it, and when we "fall in love" we go crazy over it. But does that help us find our goal of peace, harmony, balance, and contentment. When we "fall out of love" we are right back where we started or worse.

Davidji in his book *Sacred Powers* says that when we are in our mother's womb our whole reality besides our concept of being at peace, harmony, balance, and contentment is the constant beating of our mothers' heart. So, is it our mother's heartbeat that we are really looking for? When we seek love from our mother, are we trying to recreate that sense of completeness we felt in the womb? Is that love? Can our mother and father really give us the love we are seeking? After all they are only human with their own problems and emotional baggage that they may project onto us. When we discover that we must look beyond our parents we search for that perfect mate that we hope will satisfy our need for love. I have often thought that our modern-day practice of finding love in a mate is backwards. We find someone who we are physically attracted to, start a relationship, hope that it becomes an emotional relationship, and possibly in our old age, that it turns into a spiritual relationship. I believe that as a society we might have better luck starting with a spiritual bond, hope that it becomes an emotional bond, and then into a physical relationship.

Even if we do happen to find that perfect mate and even if we do have a spiritual bond with that mate, will this satisfy our ideal concept of the love we are looking for? I believe that there is only one source that can take us to that place in our heart. This is not a human source, because as humans we find it difficult to give and receive love totally unconditionally.

Before you were born you were in a divine connection with spirit. Your mother's heartbeat was the closest you could come to that state of being. When you were born you remembered that state in your deepest consciousness and you have been trying to find that connection your whole life. Regardless of your religious beliefs, you must discover for yourself your own spiritual connection to feel truly loved. When you can feel that unconditional love, love yourself.

Expanding Awareness and Consciousness

THIS CHAPTER IS DEDICATED to individual questions and observations of awareness that came to me during the quest to expand my consciousness.

What are the limits of my consciousness? I have tested the limits of my body by climbing high mountains, being extremely cold for long periods, and scuba diving deep down until my ear drums felt like they might rupture. But how can I test the limits of my consciousness when it is held captive by my mind?

To expand my consciousness, I must let go of and empty myself of everything that my ego wants to hold on to. It also requires me to see other people around me as mirrors because what I see in them is me.

I have created my whole universe based on what I have expected to see. With my eyes and heart open, I may experience unexpected wonders that will change my universe. What do I "see" when I look out? What do I "see" when you look in? What do others "see" when they look at my face?

I have been stony and solitary for many years. I ask every day to turn that stone into fertile soil to let my heart bloom so that others may want to come near enough to smell my fragrance and smile at my beauty.

At this moment, it makes no difference whether I am standing still, walking a straight line, or circling around clockwise. Everything that is happening around me visually, auditorily, aromatically, and energetically will happen. How I perceive it, how I react to it, and how and where I feel it, depends on me in this moment. I can stand with eyes closed, walk slowly and clumsily, or I can open all my senses and find my rhythm. I get to choose.

Why do I feel that I am in a constant state of sleep consciousness, when I know full well that there is a state of constant awake consciousness? Even in my deepest sleep state, even in my death state, I AM conscious.

At any given moment there are countless "Good" and "Bad" things happening around me. What I see, hear, think, and do are the external reflections of who I am inside. When all the external "Good" and "Bad" things are stripped away, who am I?

I am grateful for all my teachers, all my friends, all those who have forgiven me, all those who have been hard on me, and for that being inside of me that wants to break free of the prison of its own making so that it may Be love and be loved.

When I can completely understand and accept all my flaws, I can understand and accept the flaws in others.

I often ponder this dream between earthly birth and death, and how the experiences in this dream have expanded my consciousness and enriched my soul's journey.

If I dream of the future today, and I live in the past tomorrow, where am I now?

To stand and face my fears is the warrior's way. Silence and withdrawal are the last options when retreat is necessary. In those times, I must acknowledge that I am too weak to defend myself, rather than blame my opponent for being stronger.

How can I get to the point where I completely understand my every choice, my every decision, my every emotion, my every thought—to the point where I have absolute awareness of myself, and yet still be a part of this world?

When I die, the world will go on without me. It won't have mattered what I did for a living. It won't have mattered how much money I made, whom I knew, or how many friends I had. It won't have mattered how many people I loved or loved me. In the end, the only thing that will have mattered in my entire life is what I learned about myself in the time that I had.

Everything has its own cycle. If I can respect my own cycle, then I can respect the cycles of everything else.

There is a battle raging between the light and the dark on many levels, and while there isn't much I can do on a grand scale, I can become as aware as possible of the light and dark within and around me. I can shine my shield of light to vanquish my own shadows and be a reflection of light for others who may be living in darkness.

I know how difficult it is to stay positive with so much going wrong. It is hard to look for whatever good may come from our tragedies, but it is also rewarding. Let the light heal you as you smile at the darkness. As long as the sun can shine and the earth can spring anew, then so shall I.

Sometimes, I think of a goal as the end point, but when I reach it, I realize that it was really a starting point.

CHAPTER 14

The Gift

IN THE MOMENTS WHEN I AM GIFTED with the face of Spirit looking at me, smiling, I am in awe, in heaven, in love, smiling back. I no longer need faith or blind trust in my belief. In those moments I know beyond all doubt. And when the memory of those moments fades with the trials and the struggles of everyday life, if I am present long enough, I may be allowed that gift again.

IN THE SILENCE MUCH IS SAID,
IN THE STILLNESS THERE IS LOVE

CHAPTER 15

If I Truly Care for and Love Someone

IF I TRULY CARE FOR AND LOVE SOMEONE, I will treat them as I see them in their most positive potential. I will nourish and nurture them so that they will truly embody their positive potential no matter where it leads them, even if it leads them away from me. No matter what, I will always love and care for this person.

However, if I care more for myself in the relationship, I will see and treat the other person in the way that best fits the pattern that I have set out for them, no matter how harmful it may be for them.

How do I know if I truly love this person or if I am just using them to play out my own patterns?

I must be satisfied with my life and myself before I know this person, and I must be free from fear of losing them after we are together. I must constantly strive to maintain my emotional sovereignty.

CHAPTER 16

Secret Contracts

A SECRET CONTRACT IS A CONTRACT held between you and another person that is hidden from one or both of you. It may be buried so far below your conscious mind that you are unaware of it yourself. The contract is a rationalization for any unspoken expectations you have of the other person. Parents, siblings, spouses, children, and friends all can keep secret contracts. You may even consider a prayer to God/Spirit to be a secret contract. Below are some examples of secret contracts.

Parents to their children:
Some parents are good at expressing their expectations for the contracts they have, but some parents may think to themselves, *I_______________ (pay for you, work hard for you, cook for you, take care of you, birthed you, get up early and go to work for you, etc.), and the least you could do is _______________ (clean your room, do the dishes, show some respect, give me a break when I come home, do chores around the house, study hard in school, go to bed without so much fuss, clean up after yourself, etc.).*

Children of parents:

Family dynamics can be very complicated, and each child may not feel they are getting the attention and love they need. A child may think to themselves, *I _____________________ (will be your slave, will let you do "this" to me, will take care of this, will not say anything about this, will let you emotionally and psychologically abuse me, do anything you say, etc., for your_____________________ (love, attention, respect, kindness, acknowledgment, trust, etc.).*

Siblings:

Depending on how many children are in a family, it is almost certain that not all of the children are treated the same, and each child has their own relationship with a parent. There can be rivalry between siblings, which can turn into resentment and anger. A sibling may think to themselves, I was made to _____________________ (take care of you, be nice to you, give something I like to you, let you get all the attention, be the mediator between you and them, be silent, etc.), the least you could do is_____________________ (let me do this, be nice to me, take care of me, give me this, show me some respect, not be angry with me, love me, let me have this, etc.).

Spouses:

I believe that secret contracts may be the greatest causes of friction and divorces between spouses. A spouse may think to themselves, I _____________________ (get up early and go to work, pay for this, do all the mechanical chores, cook our meals, do all the laundry, clean up after you, mow the lawn, vacuum the house, clean the floors, let you do this to me, do everything you say, etc.), and the least you can do is ___________________(cook my meals, clean up after me, do my laundry, do what I ask you to do, let me do this to you, love me, respect me , listen to me, have a drink ready for me when I come home, have dinner ready for me when I come home, give me a break when I come home, buy this for me, take me out to dinner once a week, take care of me, etc.).

Friends:

A friend may think to themselves, I ___________________ (drop everything for you, come over, help you with this, do this for you, give you this, take care of this, listen to you, cry with you, respect you, love you, etc.,) and the least you can do is ___________________ (come over when I need you, help me with this, take care of this, listen to me, do this for me, respect me, love me, etc.).

God/Spirit:

Depending on a person's religious preferences and their level of spiritual awareness, they may have a secret contract in place all the time. A person might think to themselves, I will ___________________(be honest, be good, be nice, be faithful, be humble, hold strictly to the dogma, spread my faith, etc.) and the least you can do is ___________________ (keep me safe, keep me healthy, keep me wealthy, keep my spouse faithful, keep my children healthy and safe, keep me fed, keep my life easy, let me live a long life, etc.). A person with no religious or spiritual beliefs may be less likely to have a secret contract in place when all is going well, but as soon as something drastic comes along that person may strike up a contract and think to themselves, I will________________ (be good, be nicer, be faithful, be or do whatever you ask of me, etc.) if you will only ________________ (save my parent, save my child, save my spouse, bring me food, bring me wealth, let me buy that car/house/dress, etc.).

I was somewhere between 10 and 12 when I first made a contract with god. As a family, we had gone skiing during the winter at Stevens Pass. At that time, there were three rope tows going up a very steep mountain. Each successive rope tow was faster and harder to get up. As a child I had to hold onto the rope very tightly. I even had a clamping device that grabbed onto the rope to make it easier to hold on. Even with this device, children on their own were not heavy enough to keep the rope at ground level. As the rope towed me up the mountain, it lifted me up in the air—as high as five feet at one point. I remember asking god to let me get up to the top of the last rope tow at least half the times I tried. I don't remember what I promised, but I'm sure I promised something. I was also trying hard and I thought that might be enough.

When you see secret contracts, you may have had or still do have, you will have to decide what to do about them. It is helpful to at least acknowledge them and try to understand their consequences. You might even vocalize your expectations and dissolve the contracts you hold, or simply let go of any expectations you hold for what you have done.

CHAPTER 17

How to Bring Energy into a Room

My goal is to act appropriately with all people at all times. But I either act prematurely when I want something too much, or I let opportunities slip by when I don't want them badly enough. I am a warrior in training, and I do battle with myself as I learn.

EVERYONE IS DIFFERENT. Everyone has a different personality, or what I call their own Energy Signature. Some people use the zodiac signs or other personality tests to determine where they fit in on the personality palette. Some people are considered introverts and other are extroverts. Some people may be a mix depending on whether they are in their element, or their knowledge level on a particular subject.

I would never discount any of the above, but when someone comes into a room, I only see their energy signature. Do they come in quietly and wait until they are spoken to first? Do they come in fast while talking and gesturing with their hands? Are they too loud? Do they seem calm or agitated? Does it feel like they are bragging? Does it feel like they are being honest and sincere? Do they start talking and never seem to stop? Do they interrupt others who try to talk? Are they silent and reserved? Do they come in, get what they want, and leave? Do they come in and instantly start telling you how bad their life is?

Whether a person is aware of these situations on a conscious level or not, I believe we are all aware on a subconscious or feeling level. How do you feel after being with someone who exhibits any of the above characteristics? Now ask yourself, how do others feel about you? How do you want others to feel about you? I am not asking anyone to change who they are. It is up to you to understand yourself and to determine for yourself if you would like to do anything differently. The next time you walk into your own home, a friend's house, or a party, take a second to see how you feel about yourself. As soon as you step into the house, take moment to notice how you feel about yourself now.

CHAPTER 18

Energy Boundary Basics

1. There is a way to help you determine the limits of your personal energy. Stand up and hold your arms and hands out in front of you. Now visualize a distance 6 to 12 inches out farther than your hands. At that distance, draw a circle all the way around your body. Whether in your own home, in a crowd, or out on the street, you should consider this to be the maximum limit of your personal energy. If you imagine everyone's energy extended to this point, you can clearly see how people's energies can overlap. We feel this overlap when someone gets too close to us, so when you go into someone else's space, imagine how your energy might affect them.

2. Your thoughts and your energy can be felt on some level even if you don't know it on a conscious level. It is important to keep this in mind when you are angry, resentful, or frustrated with someone. They can feel your energy whether you are in the same room or not. I have found that if someone is angry with me, I can either respond with more anger, which changes nothing, or I can respond with forgiveness and understanding, and something will change for the better.

3. It is very important to understand that anyone who pushes their energy outside of their own energetic boundary to influence someone else in a negative way is performing a form of sorcery, and they are only adding to their own negative Karma. Any form of energy manipulation, whether it is emotional, physical, or spiritual, will add to a person's Karma.

4. When a person is in a room by themselves, they can take up the whole house with their energy. They can sing, yell, dance, and do whatever they want to do. As long as the neighbors don't complain, they have only themselves to please. If another person enters the house, they should then limit their energy output by one half. If a third person enters the house, they should then limit their energy output by one third. If there is a large crowd in the house, they will have to determine what their energy output should be. In a math format, the total energy output in a house should equal 100%. If there were 10 people in the house, then each person should not put out more than 10%. Each person should be given an opportunity to take up their share of energetic space in the house. If one person in the house dominates all the energy, I can guarantee that others will feel resentful, frustrated, or angry.

5. When you are in a conversation, it is important to give everyone an equal share of the conversational energy. When people who are not given the chance to talk, they can become resentful, frustrated, or angry.

6. There are two very basic energy signatures that are apparent, and which can determine someone's personal, social, and political outlook and preferences. A person may have the energy signature of "I, Me, Mine," or a person may have the energy signature of "We, Us, Ours." These two signatures can be very telling of the person's approach to life.

He felt no fear of death. Instead, what came into his mind was the realization that each and every moment of this life must be felt as if it is happening in slow motion and to its fullest, because a person never knows when death may happen.

CHAPTER 19

Once Upon a Time

ONCE UPON A TIME, long, long ago, there was a young man of 21. A complicated chain of events had led him to being alone, without family or friends in a foreign Stone Age country. A country with dirt roads, thatched huts, rice paddies, lots of rats, and a scarcity of dogs because they were used as a source of meat.

What makes a person who they are? Is it what they experienced in childhood? Or is there something else that is inherently in the person—something that, no matter what, drives them to be who they are? Already in his life, this young man had been forced into being responsible for his three siblings. He excelled in outdoor activities where his only competition was with nature and himself. He never belonged to any sports groups or teams. He felt uncomfortable being around more than a few people at a time and could only do so for short periods of time before needing to leave. So, it would come as no surprise that when this young man was in a foreign country, he did not spend much time connecting with any one group.

In the 16 months he spent there, he stayed in many different places. Often in a single evening he would travel from one group of partiers to the next, sometimes visiting as many as four or five before heading back to his bunk. The problem with going to so many different parties was that each party might have a different mode of intoxification. He would start out drinking with one group, then smoking pot with the next, maybe take LSD with the next one, or smoke hash and drink with the next. One night, this very high young man quite suddenly found himself waking up from a blackout alone on a dirt road on a pitch-black dark night. He chose a direction that felt right and walked ahead as if he could see until he sensed that he was not alone on this road and stopped. The ground on his left was road-level. He could smell the sea. The ground on his right was a bank that cut upwards a little higher than his head. When he turned his head to the right, he could see two very still cat-like eyes shining at him. He froze, staring at these eyes for what felt like a long time, but was more likely only a few seconds. Whether real or imagined, the cat pounced at his head and he raised his arms up to protect himself. He felt no fear of death. Instead, what came into his mind was the realization that each and every moment of this life must be felt as if it is happening in slow motion and to its fullest, because a person never knows when death may happen.

To this day, the young man, who has now grown old, does not fear death. He sees his life as a series of moments of awareness strung together making up his time here on earth. He sees many people moving through their everyday, normal life experiences, as people operating in blackout conscious states who have yet to wake up and see what their lives are all about. He finds it uncomfortable to be around people who live like they are the ghosts of their past experiences. He once told me that it was similar to being the only sober person in a room full of drinkers who have drunk too much. He knows that there is no one to blame and nothing to do but to continue the journey and to learn as much as he can with the time he has left—which, interestingly, is just about 21 years. Knowing this, he has started his countdown, and will live with as much *intentional awareness* as possible; enjoying the moments of his life as though time were standing still just long enough for him to see and appreciate each one.

Spiritual

A S WITH THE CHAPTER on Expanding Awareness and Consciousness, the statements below came to me during times of meditation and contemplation. I offer them to you as they came to me.

"I am now thought itself stripped of all restlessness;
I am alone and constant; I am without a body or birth;
I only am the essence of being; I am the ultimate truth."

~ Atma Prabuddha, *The Upanishads*

Can you imagine a reality where you have cleansed and healed all the wounds inflicted upon your heart and soul? Can you imagine for a second that what was said and done to you by other people was about them and not ever really about you? Can you imagine your absolute forgiveness towards them, for they knew not what they did to you? Be again as the innocent child you once were.

I have seen and experienced that the "I AM" and Spirit are the co-creators of my reality. My experiences and all my triggers are of my own doing. I, along with Spirit, am responsible for where and who "I AM." The messenger is not the other. The messenger is me.

Before I was here, I was in a place that had neither time nor dimension. There was no land, no sea, and no sky. There was not even a horizon. There was only a great golden glow surrounding me, stretching away to infinity on every side, warm and so bright that it dazzled my eyes. I could see nothing but its radiance. (These words are similar to what Ben Bova said in "Vengeance of Orion," but I already knew these words before I read them). To be in such a place can be related to the Hindu concept of "Existence-Consciousness-Bliss," but to consciously leave such a place and return to Earth is the real mystery of life on Earth.

Divine death comes not to those who hold on to nothing.

Everything exists and it is all one. Everything in its most basic form is but one cell in the consciousness of Divine Spirit.

Which is more important to you, the survival of your body, or the survival of your soul?

There is a lot of uncertainty in the world today. Many countries are in states of chaos and division. I know that I have a choice—

I can react and be a part of the chaos and division of the outer world, or I can choose to calm my own inner chaos and division from SPIRIT. I choose to discover and heal the rifts within my own soul, because when there is no more chaos or division within me, there will be no more chaos or division around me.

We are not separate. Your suffering is my suffering. What can we do? Can we allow love and forgiveness into our hearts? For as long as we continue to prefer to hold anger and revenge in our hearts, there can be no healing.

Be as if blind to all judgement, fear, and separation from others. See and feel only their innocence and vulnerability. Love them.

In times past, I have felt the grip of darkness exerting its power over my soul, but when I increased the radiance of my light, the darkness had nothing to hold to.

We mourn our earthly losses with our earthly hearts, but within our heart of hearts there is joy at the knowing of the soul who is, was, and always will be, with us.

Today, as with every day, I will breath in and breath out with a smile, with hope, and with faith in myself. I will follow the yellow brick road one step at a time as I go through this thing we call life. I will listen for the voice of the Wizard of Oz as I walk with courage, with heart, with a brain, and with determination. I will watch myself on the stage as I act out my roles. Most importantly, I will sit in the theater eating popcorn, laughing and learning about all the conflicting forces within me. When the final curtain closes and I find myself walking down the aisle for the last time, I will breathe in and breathe out with a smile, with hope, and with faith as I listen to the voice of the Wizard of Oz.

CHAPTER 21

Poetry

WHEN YOU *LIVE IN SPIRIT,* everything is poetry. Every moment in which I am aware is poetry. Feelings of joy, beauty, pain, sadness, loneliness, and ecstatic bliss all roll together into oneness within. Sometimes to be expressed. Sometimes to be felt. Always to be appreciated.

I sit in spring and watch as the grass grows.
I know it is calling me and I will soon have to
heed that call.
But, for the moment I am content to sip my tea and
watch it grow and watch all of our Mother giving
birth again like nothing else matters.
I take notice, then I act.

Snow-capped hills, fields of green.
What on earth could it mean.
A goose walking in step behind a llama.
I love it when friendship is seen.

Wet, wet, wet, wild, wild, wild, my sailboat rocks.
I am safe inside.

The sun is bright and warm above the chill air.

Early morning darkness, wet, windy, cold,
I am drawn in and head down. Stop!
Frogs croaking with delight. Shift!
Head up, smile open, I croak with delight.
Beauty joy bliss.

Early evening gray drops of rain cleansing.
Seas gray, green, white at the tug's brow.
Silent tears wash and heal the chords just cut.
There is still a Sun. There is still a smile.

The morning sunrise, magnificent shades and
layers of white, gray, pink, rose, orange, blue.
Textures and depths of clouds flowing past.
Positively alive, beautiful, smile provoking in the
moment.

The Heron stands patiently in the still water.
It watches its own reflection until some movement
catches its eye then acts exactly as needed in the
moment.
The human watching thinks this Heron must be
a true warrior.
The Heron remains standing patiently in
the still water.

Three buzzards circle overhead.
Makes me wonder, "am I dead?"
If I am alive, what rules this being?
Is it my heart or is it my head?
I ponder as I drive ever forward, one-wheel turn
at a time.

Rolling fields of spring green grass,
Gray white clouds hanging low,
Feeding geese waddling slow.

A lonely crow on a post,
Standing still ready to fly,
Looking down, wondering why,
Fiercely Caws with head up high,

Caw who, Caw am, Caw I,
Turns its head gliding off
Caw I, Caw am, Caw I.

Of all there is known and unknown there is
only one heart beating.
Spirit heart beats forever,
Love when hearts beat together,
Physical hearts come and go,
Let your heart beat with me.

Judge not the moon for only the moon
knows the moon.
Yet the moon sees itself not,
but only as its reflection and its shadow from
the light of the sun.

There is only one Om Oming, Om with it,
There is only one Heart beating, beat with it,
There is only one Breath breathing, breathe with it,
There is only one Stillness, be still with it,
There is only one Oneness, be one with it.

With patience, allowance and trust, we are seen
by those who have eyes to see;
We are heard by those who have ears to hear;
We are felt by those who have the heart to feel;
We are served by those who are ready to serve;
We serve those who are ready to be served.

I watch the morning dawn from darkness slowly
bringing the light which shines bright until it slowly
fades back to darkness. I breathe in, hold, rest, and
breathe out, hold, rest, and breathe in.
I lay my head down, close my eyes and fall into sleep.
I become aware of myself as I open my eyes awake.
I remember, I forget, I remember, I forget.
I watch the seasons of the earth awaken into one
season and move onto the next.
I have a body that exists, I no longer have a body that
exists, I have a body that exists, I no longer have a
body that exists.
I am here, I am there, I am everywhere, I am nowhere.
No matter the time, the space, or the place; no matter
who or where or when I am; I will always be in the
middle of the existence of everything and at the same
time in the middle of the existence of nothing.
I am the past, I am the future, I am the present.
Who am I?

Sipping a holiday wine. Your color, aroma, and taste.
The feel of you in my hand.
Are you as I dreamed? Are you as I hoped?
Are you what I have longed for?
You are savored for a moment for the wine
that you are.
My experience of you transported into memory.

CHAPTER 22

In Closing

I STARTED THIS BOOK talking about using the natural desire for adventure in our lives in our search for peace and happiness. What I didn't talk about was the second part of our desire for adventure. Do you remember when you were a child on your first big adventures or later in your adult life when you went on that exotic vacation for the first time? What was it about that experience that sparked you? I believe it is the thrill of discovery. We probably can't remember how thrilled we were when we took our first step, but we might remember the exhilaration of our first kiss. The thrill of discovery is what drives our desire for adventure.

This book is all about discovery, but a discovery of the hidden world that resides just below the surface of our everyday consciousness. When we were young, we may not have worried so much whether our adventure was a success or a failure because the thrill of the discovery was more important. But when we are older and our egos become more important to us than the discovery itself, we may be afraid to look at what is just below our surface. The fear of disturbing our ego may hinder our adventurous spirit and keep us from the discovery that we are looking for.

For some reason, we have been taught to relate our ego with our self-esteem. We have been taught to fear failure because failure will diminish our ego and lower our self-esteem. If we continue to fear failure to the point that it restricts our learning and to always need to be right, then we really have failed, and we may never learn anything new that might lead us to that place we are searching for.

I believe that what we were taught about our ego equaling our level of self esteem is not accurate. Our ego is based on what our mind is telling us who we are and, our self-esteem is based on what our heart is telling us who we are. We need our ego and its sense of survival on a physical level, but when it comes to changing who we are inside, trust your heart. It takes courage to change, but it can be an exciting adventure full of thrilling discoveries.

MAY THE GREAT BRIGHT LIGHT
ILLUMINATE YOUR PATH
TO PEACE AND HARMONY
AND BRING COSMIC BALANCE
TO YOUR SOUL

About the Author

DAVID LADD is a retired civil servant with an additional 10 years as a school bus driver. He started his adventurous life learning to snow ski at 5 years old and scuba diving at 13. Because of his adventurous parents, he spent summers hiking and camping throughout the Pacific Northwest wilderness and clam digging along the Washington coast. As an adult he turned to mountain climbing which took him to high elevation mountains in North America, Mexico, South America, and Africa. He has traveled to many countries investigating ancient ruins and pyramids from both sides of the Atlantic. For the last 15 years he has traveled throughout the Pacific Northwest San Juan islands and Canadian Gulf islands in his sailboat. He has studied and immersed himself in many different energy healing modalities to help others and himself.